God, He is Poetry

LONETTA TAYLOR

To order additional copies of this book, contact:
Xlibris Corporation
1-888-795-4274
www.Xlibris.com
Orders@Xlibris.com
114560

Contents

GOD

HE IS POETRY

I Write Poetry

I WRITE POETRY BECAUSE GOD HAVE BEEN SO GOOD TO ME,
I EXPRESS MYSELF BECAUSE HE FULFILLS ALL MY NEEDS.

MOST OF THE WORDS THAT COMES TO MIND,
IT'S MY LIFE OF SEEING WHAT GOES ON IN TIME.

LIFE IS POETRY TO ME AND I CAN UNDERSTAND,
THAT WHAT HAPPENS IN LIFE IS NOT CREATED BY MAN.

THE LIFE OF OTHERS, THE SADNESS, THE LOVE, THE CHILDREN,
FITS IN MY TREND OF THOUGHT,
THE WORDS GOD PLACED IN MY MIND IS A PRICE
THAT CAN'T BE BOUGHT.

SOME PEOPLE DON'T RHYME IN POETRY, BUT I DO.
I GUESS YOU CAN SAY THAT I'M JUST OLD SCHOOL.

WHATEVER A PERSON WRITE IS DIFFERENT FROM MINE,
I'M JUST A POETRY WRITER WHO LIKES TO RHYME.

LONETTA TAYLOR

A Thankful Prayer

THANK YOU LORD FOR LETTING US SEE ANOTHER DAY,
THANK YOU LORD FOR TAKING SOME OF OUR PAINS AWAY.

THANK YOU LORD FOR LAST NIGHT OF SLEEP,
AND WHEN WE AWOKE THIS MORNING,
YOU LIFTED OUR SOULS TO
KEEP.

LEAD US THIS DAY WITH A SMILE ON OUR FACE,
AND GIVE US ENCOURAGEMENT TO HELP
OTHERS RUN THIS CHRISTIAN
RACE.

TO GO ABOUT OUR BUSINESS TO THE END OF THE DAY,
HOPING TO FIND A QUIET SPOT NOW AND THEN TO PRAY.

THE STORM IS NOT QUITE OVER FOR US YOU SEE!
SO KEEP A PRAYER IN OUR HEARTS,
AND THE LORD WILL TAKE CARE
OF OUR NEEDS.

WE KNOW PRAYER HAVE BROUGHT US THROUGH THUS FAR,
SO PRAY THE LORD WILL KEEP US SAFE
NO MATTER WHO, OR WHERE
WE ARE.

WHEN WE RETIRE LORD TO OUR RESTING PLACE TONIGHT.
PRAY THE LORD WILL LET YOU SEE
ANOTHER DAY OF HIS MARVELOUS LIGHT.

Dedication

THERE ARE A FEW PEOPLE THAT HAVE BEEN
INSPIRING IN MY LIFE,
THAT'S YOU PASTOR KENNEDY C. LUCKETT, AND
YOUR LOVELY WIFE.

EACH SABBATH IS A JOY FOR ME AT MAGAZINE
SEVEN DAY ADVENTIST CHURCH,
I TAKE IT AT HEART, AND WHAT IT IS WORTH.

THIS BOOK OF POEMS IS DEDICATED TO YOU, MY
HUSBAND, AND MY MOM WHO HAVE PASSED AWAY,
SHE WOULD HAVE BEEN PROUD OF ME, AND I HOPE
TO HEAR HER SAY THIS TO ME ONE DAY.

A Helping Hand

WHAT A JOY AND A PLEASURE IT IS TO KNOW,
GOD PLACED YOU IN OUR LIVES A FEW YEARS AGO.

WE WHERE NOT IN THE TRUTH AND WAS LOST ABOUT GOD'S
PLAN,
BUT HE'S ALWAYS THERE TO SEND A HELPING HAND.

YOU ARE THAT HAND THAT LIFTED OUR SPIRITS UP,
THE KINDNESS YOU SHOWED, WE COULDN'T GET ENOUGH.

TO BE TAUGHT THROUGH THE SEMINARS ON A SPIRITUAL
LEVEL,
NONE COULD GET CLOSE, NOT EVEN THE DEVIL.

RALPH YOU ARE TRULY A FRIEND, AND A TRUE BROTHER,
IT'S GONNA BE HARD TO REPLACE YOU, WE CAN THINK OF NO
OTHER!

YOU WILL ALWAYS BE ON THE TAYLORS MIND AND HEART,
NO MATTER WHERE YOU ARE, IT'S JUST THE DISTANCE APART.

BRINGING ME AND MY HUSBAND TOGETHER ON ONE ACCORD,
THANK YOU, GOD BLESS YOU BROTHER RALPH FORD.

I HOPE YOU AND YOU FAMILY WILL KEEP IN TOUCH,
WE LOVE YOU ALL, AND WILL MISS YOU VERY MUCH.

ALVIN AND LONETTA TAYLOR

Jesus Is Alive

JESUS IS SO ALIVE IN OUR HEARTS TODAY,
YOU MAY NOT SEE HIM, BUT YOU CAN FEEL HIM
IN A SPIRITUAL WAY,

HIS DEATH ON THE CROSS WAS ENOUGH TO BEAR,
NOW HE HAS RISEN TO SHOW HOW MUCH HE CARES.

ONE DAY OUT OF THE YEAR, ON EASTER DAY
IT'S A CELEBRATION FOR SOME, IN A BIG WAY.

EVERYDAY SHOULD BE A SPECIAL DAY OF PRAISING THE LORD.
IN THE MORNING, IN THE EVENING AND AT NIGHT.
IT'S NOT AT ALL HARD!

THERE SHOULD BE NO SPECIAL TIME OF DAY THAT WE DO THIS,
THE JOY THAT COMES, IS A TIME YOU DON'T WANT TO MISS.

WE DRESS UP, WE BUY CANDY TO PUT IN A EASTER BASKET,
NEVER REFLECTING HOW JESUS DIED,
AND HOW HE WAS REJECTED.

SOME TAKE THIS DAY FOR GRANTED,
NOT THINKING WHAT JESUS WENT THROUGH.
HE SUFFERED AND DIED ON THE CROSS! FOR ME AND YOU.

THE BIBLE TELLS YOU THE REASON WHY WE CELEBRATE THIS DAY.
CELEBRATE AS YOU DO, BUT THERE IS A BETTER WAY.

Keep On Praying

JUST LIKE ME I BE PRAYING A LOT,
NOT JUST PRAYING IN ONE PARTICULAR SPOT.

THERE IS A PLENTY ON MY MIND,
BUT SURELY THESE THINGS WILL WORK OUT IN TIME.

SO MUCH IS GOING ON IN THIS WORLD TODAY,
YOU HAVE TO PRAY TO KEEP THE DEVIL AWAY.

SOMEONE IS ALWAYS TRYING TO STEAL YOUR JOY,
WORKING YOUR NERVES TO THE VERY LAST CORE.

YOUR RESPONSE IS TO PRAY AND PRAY AGAIN,
SAY TO THEM, "STEP AWAY SATAN, YOU CAN'T MAKE ME BEND.

"THE FATHER SAID", THIS TO SHALL PASS.
ONE DAY YOU WILL BE, FREE AT LAST!

YOU CAN'T GO A DAY WITHOUT PRAYING IN HIS NAME,
IT WOULD BE A DAY OF KNOWING IT'S A SHAME.

IT WOULD BE A DAY OF LIKE BEING TOTALLY LOST,
PUT THE TIME TO USE, DO NOT TURN HIM OFF.

TIME IS RUNNING OUT FOR US,
PUTTING OUR TRUST IN GOD IS A MUST!

Flowers Of Praise

ON THIS SPECIAL DAY OF GIVING YOU THE PRAISE,
SISTER GLADYS SWAIN, WE THANK GOD FOR YOU,
IN HIS HOLY NAME.

SOME OF US HAVE COME AND GONE,
BUT BY THE GRACE OF GOD, YOU KEEP HOLD ON.

YOU'VE BEEN LIKE A FIXTURE IN THIS CHURCH FROM THE BEGINNING
OF TIME,
GOD PLACED YOU HERE, AND YOU LET YOUR
LITTLE LIGHT SHINE.

HOW CAN WE NOT LOVE A SWEET LADY LIKE YOU,
YOU GIVE THE LORD PRAISE IN ALL THAT YOU DO.

GRACE AND PEACE BE MULTIPLIED UNTO YOU,
GOD GRANT THIS ALSO FOR THE FAMILY TOO.

KEEP ON KEEPING ON TILL THE SAVIOUR COMES,
YOUR REWARD WILL COME FROM THE FATHER AND THE SON.

Believe

EVERYTHING IS GOING TO WORK OUT RIGHT,
BELIEVE IN GOD, WITH ALL YOUR MIGHT.

DARK CLOUD MAY COME, BUT WILL GO AWAY.
AND WE WILL SEE A BRIGHTER DAY.

SOMETIMES IT SEEM THINGS ARE NOT GOING TO
WORK OUT FOR YOU,
PRAY TO THE HEAVENLY FATHER, HE KNOWS WHAT TO DO.

WHAT A BETTER WAY TO LIFT YOUR SPIRITS UP,
AFTER YOU HAVE HAD A DRINK FROM THE BITTER CUP.

DON'T EXPECT THINGS TO GO RIGHT ON THIS EARTH,
BUT BELIEVE ONE DAY THE LORD WILL GIVE YOU A NEW BIRTH.

"HE SAID", BELIEVE IN HIM AND TRUST IN HIM,
THIS TO SHALL PAST,
THESE TRAIL THAT YOU'RE GOING THROUGH,
WILL ONE DAY BE YOUR LAST.

Have Faith

WHEN LIFE'S PROBLEMS WEIGH YOU DOWN,
AND YOU'RE DOWN TO
YOUR LAST ROPE.
CALL ON THE SAVIOR TO HELP, FOR HE'S OUR ONLY HOPE!

THE STEPS WE MUST TAKE SEEMS HARD TO EXCEPT,
HIS PROMISES AND HIS WORD, HAS HE NOT KEPT?

WHEN HE'S NOT THERE AND AT YOUR CONVENIENCE,
JUST BE PATIENT AND WAIT, AND BE A LITTLE LENIENT.

YOU'RE NOT THE ONLY ONE WHO NEEDS SOME HELP,
NOW AND THEN,
HE WILL ONLY COME WHEN THE TIME IS RIGHT, FOR HE'S OUR
TRUSTED FRIEND.

I KNOW AT TIMES IT SEEMS AS IF HE DOESN'T CARE,
BUT THINK OF ALL THE OTHER TIMES WHEN
YOU CALLED, WASN'T HE
THERE?

WHEN WE PRAY AND WAIT FOR BLESSINGS GOD
PROMISES TO GIVE'
WE NOW KNOW WHAT WE MUST DO IN ORDER
TO SURVIVE AND LIVE.

Take Control Lord

LORD TAKE CONTROL OF MY BODY, AND MY MIND,
LET ME STAY FOCUS, ON YOU ALL THE TIME.

PLEASE LET ME NOT THINK OF THE PAIN I'M GOING THROUGH,
LET ME THINK ONLY ON THE FAITH, AND THE BLESSINGS YOU DO.

DAY AFTER DAY IT SEEMS LIKE A TEST,
THROUGH ALL OF THIS LORD, YOU KNOW WHAT IS BEST.

I'M GOING TO KEEP ON PRAYING AS I GO THROUGH THIS,
I PRAY WHEN THE TIME COMES I'LL BE ONE ON YOUR LIST.

ONE DAY ALL THIS SUFFERING AND PAIN WILL BE GONE,
I PRAY LORD YOU WILL EXCEPT ME IN YOUR HEAVENLY HOME.

A HOME WHERE I KNOW THERE IS HEALING POWER,
LIKE A ROSE THAT TURNS INTO A BEAUTIFUL FLOWER.

NO MORE DOCTORS, NO MORE MEDICINE, NO MORE BILLS,
I CAN'T WAIT,
MY JESUS WILL BE WAITING FOR ME AT THE PEARLY GATE.

WHEN YOU CALL MY NAME LORD I'LL BE HAPPY AS CAN BE,
I KNOW THAT IN YOUR LOVING ARMS, I WILL BE FREE.

God's Light

GOD'S LIGHT IS FOR ALL TO SEE,
HE CREATED THE WORLD FOR YOU AND ME!

WITH HIS LOVE AND US IN MIND,
HE GAVE HIS SON FOR ALL MANKIND.

HE HAS PROVEN HIS POWER TO US ON END,
GOD LET'S US KNOW THAT WE HAVE A FRIEND.

HE WILL NOT LEAVE US IN THE DARKEST NIGHT,
GOD WILL PROVIDE US WITH HIS BEAUTIFUL LIGHT.

WE LOOK TO THE DAYLIGHT TO THE HEAVEN'S ABOVE,
THIS WAS A CREATION OF GOD'S PURE LOVE.

WE LOOK TO THE HEAVENS IN THE DARK OF THE NIGHT,
BUT WE KNOW IN THE MORNING, THE SUN WILL SHINE BRIGHT.

Try Jesus

WHEN LIFE'S PROBLEM WEIGH YOU DOWN,
AND YOU SAY YOU HAVE
DONE YOUR BEST,
DON'T GET ANGRY AND BLAME SOMEONE ELSE, FOR THIS IS ONLY A
TEST.

HE GIVES YOU ALL THE CHANCES LIKE HE GIVE EVERYONE ELSE,
IT'S TIME TO STAND UP, AND STEP UP,
STOP THINKING ONLY OF SELF.

LAST WEEK HE GAVE YOU A BLESSING, AND YOU USED IT,
IN SPITE OF YOURSELF,
AGAIN THIS WEEK YOU NEED HIM AGAIN,
YOU'RE ALWAYS CRYING FOR HELP!.

DID YOU THANK HIM, DID YOU PRAISE HIM, FOR THE BLESSINGS
HE ALREADY GAVE,
OR DID YOU TAKE IT FOR GRANTED?, GOD DOESN'T
WORK THAT WAY.

HE SAID, "HE WOULD POUR YOU OUT ALL THE BLESSINGS THAT
YOU'LL EVER NEED",
BUT HAVE YOU EVER DONE SOMETHING FOR SOMEONE ELSE,
HAVE YOU EVER DONE A GOOD DEED.

WHEN THE TIME IS RIGHT, GOD WILL TAKE CARE OF YOUR NEEDS,
BUT GOD EXPECTS YOU TO BE FAITHFUL, BEFORE HE PLANTS ANY
SEEDS.

LOVE HIM, TRUST HIM, GOD'S WORD IS TRUE,
TRY HIM, DO AS HE SAYS, AND HE'LL TAKE CARE OF YOU.

A Prayer

LORD KEEP US IN YOUR PRECIOUS HANDS,
PLEASE LET THIS BE YOUR BLESSED DEMAND.

LORD! PLEASE KEEP THE DEVIL AWAY,
LEST WE WILL GO ASTRAY.

I PRAY FOR PEACE EACH AND EVERY DAY,
THIS WORLD NEEDS IT IN A BIG, BIG WAY.

IF WE ALL PRAY AND ASK FROM YOU,
THERE'S NO MATTER WHAT YOU MAY DO!

YOU HAVE A HEART OF PURE GOLD,
LOOKING TO YOU, OUR FAITH WILL UNFOLD.

PLEASE GIVE US STRENGTH, AND FAITH THIS DAY,
OUR FATHER WE DO PRAY.

(JAN. 6, 2005)

Thank The Lord For Everyday

DEAR GOD IN HEAVEN THANK YOU SO
FOR MAKING TREES AND FLOWERS GROW.

FOR ANIMALS BOTH BIG AND SMALL,
FOR SUMMER, WINTER, SPRING, AND FALL.

FOR MAKING DAY AND MAKING NIGHT,
AND FOR THE SUN THAT SHINES SO BRIGHT.

THANK YOU FOR MY FAMILY,
AND THANKS SO MUCH FOR MAKING ME.

Trust Him

WHEN MY SOUL WAS SINKING DOWN IN SIN,
I CALL ON A SOURCE THAT CAN LOOK DEEP WITHIN.

HE CHANGED MY LIFE, AND MY DARKEST NIGHT,
HE WILL FILL YOUR SOUL WITH PURE DELIGHT.

HE IS CALLED BY A LOTS OF NAMES,
I CALL HIM JESUS, BUT HIS HEART REMAINS THE SAME.

THERE IS NO OTHER MAN THAT I CAN CALL ON,
YOU CAN KNEEL IN PRAYER BENEATH HIS THRONE.

I NEED TO KEEP THE DEVIL AWAY,
HIS ANSWER IS TO READ HIS WORD, AND PRAY.

I SAY LORD, IT'S SO HARD IN THIS WORLD OF
TRIALS AND TRIBULATION.
HE SAID HE'S COMING SOON, JUST READ HIS BOOK OF
REVELATION.

THE BEST THING FOR US TO DO, IS GET OUR LIFE STRAIGHT.
THAT IS THE ONLY WAY TO ENTER, THE PEARLY GATES.

So Thankful

THROUGH THE YEARS, WE HAVE SO MUCH TO BE THANKFUL FOR,
WHETHER YOU THINK SO OR NOT.
GOD HAS GIVEN YOU A LOTS IN YOUR LIFETIME
SURELY YOU HAVEN'T
FORGOT!

AS YOU WHERE GROWING UP' IT WASN'T EASY TO SURVIVE
DID GOD NOT LIFT YOU UP AND STEP IN ON TIME?

THEN AS AN ADULT THERE WAS TRAILS AND TRIBULATIONS,
THIS WAS MORE ADDED AGGRAVATIONS.

YOU MUST HAVE FAITH IN THE LORD,
FOR YOU MADE IT THROUGH,
KEEP TRUSTING IN THE LORD, FOR THERE IS
NOTHING HE WANT DO
FOR YOU.

Prayers Answered

I CALLED ON THE LORD TODAY, AND ASKED HIM TO HAVE HIS WAY!
I DIDN'T KNOW WHAT TO SAY, BECAUSE MY MIND WASN'T FOCUSED ON
TO PRAY.

IT WAS ME WHO HAD A LOTS ON MY MIND, AND COULDN'T THINK I WAS
NOT WELL AT THE TIME.

WHEN YOUR THOUGHTS ARE NOT WHERE IT'S SUPPOSE TO BE,
DEPRESSED, DOWN, AND NOT KNOWING THERE WAS A NEED.

I FINALLY REALIZED NOW IS THE TIME TO CALL ON HIM,
FOR MY LIGHT WAS GETTING A LITTLE DIM.

NOT THINKING MY PRAYERS WOULD BE ANSWERED NOW,
I DIDN'T HAVE MY HEAD HEAVEN BOUND.

GETTING DOWN ON MY KNEES AND SAYING LORD
YOUR CHILD NEEDS
YOU,
MY HEART IS HEAVY AND I DON'T KNOW WHAT TO DO.

THEN I CALLED ON HIM WITH MY REQUEST,
THE LORD SET MY SOUL AT REST.

MY FAITH WAS TAKEN AWAY FOR AWHILE,
GOD BROUGHT IT BACK, AND NOW I CAN SMILE.

IF EVER IN DOUBT JUST CALL ON HIS NAME,
LEAVE IT TO OUR FATHER, AND YOUR LIFE WILL CHANGE.

Be Grateful For The Little Things

BE GRATEFUL FOR THE LITTLE THINGS THAT MAKES EACH DAY
WORTHWHILE,
A FRIEND WHO BRINGS YOU FLOWERS,
A LOVED ONE WARMING SMILE.

REMEMBER TO COUNT YOUR BLESSINGS, HOWEVER BIG OR SMALL,
THEY'RE THE SILVER LINING, WHENEVER STORM CLOUDS FALL.

APPRECIATE THE MOMENTS SHARED WITH FRIENDS AND FAMILY,
AS YOU PRAY FOR OTHERS OR JUST SIP A CUP OF TEA.

TAKE TIME TO SEND OUT "THANK YOUS" OR A GIFT
YOU MAY RECEIVE,
OR SEND A CARD OF ENCOURAGEMENTS, WHEN THOSE YOU KNOW
MIGHT GRIEVE.

IT'S THE LITTLE THINGS WE SAY OR DO THAT
PAYS THE BIG DIVIDENDS,
WHEN WE COUNT OUR BLESSINGS, WITH GOD,
THERE IS NO END.

IT ONLY TAKES A HUG OR TWO TO GENERATE A SMILE.
BE GRATEFUL FOR THE LITTLE THINGS THAT MAKE EACH DAY
WORTHWHILE.

God Still Reigns

SOMETIMES OUR SICKNESS TAKES US DOWN FOR AWHILE,
BUT BELIEVE IN FAITH, AND SAY I'M GODS CHILD!.

LIVING IN A WORLD NEVER KNOWING WHAT WILL HAPPEN NEXT,
LOOK UP FOR STRENGTH, FOR ONLY GOD KNOWS WHAT IS BEST.

IF YOU'RE FAITHFUL, LOVING AND BELIEVE GOD WILL SEE YOU
THROUGH,
THEN BELIEVE ONE DAY GOD WILL MAKE YOU BRAND NEW.

WHEN THE SAVIOUR COMES AND TAKE US HOME,
ALL THESE DISEASES, SICKNESS, AND PAIN WILL BE GONE.

STAY PRAYERFUL, AND HANG ON IN THERE MY FRIEND,
FOR ONE JOYOUS DAY, THIS WILL ALL END.

WE HAVE TO STAY FAITHFUL, NO MATTER WHAT IT TAKES.
THAT IF YOU WANT TO SEE OUR SAVIOUR FACE TO FACE.

OH! WHAT A GLORIOUS DAY THIS WILL BE,
WHEN YOU ARE HEALTHY, HAPPY, AND FREE.

AND WHEN THE HEAVENLY GATES OPEN WIDE FOR YOU,
GOD'S ANGELS WILL GUIDE YOU ON THROUGH.

AND JUST TO WALK DOWN THE STREETS OF PURE GOLD,
AND TO SEE ALL THE BEAUTIFUL THINGS THE BIBLE TOLD.

THIS IS A PLACE YOU WILL LIVE FOREVER,
THIS IS THE PLACE YOU WANTED TO GO: CALLED HEAVEN.

10/19/2010

Sing Praises

SING HALLELUJAH TO GOD ABOVE,
FOR HE IS WORTHY TO BE PRAISED, SO SHOW HIM LOVE.

NO OTHER SHOULD WE LIFT OUR VOICES HIGH,
WITH OUR HEADS LOOKING UP TO THE SKY.

THANK HIM FOR ALL HE HAS DONE FOR US,
SINGING PRAISES TO OUR SAVIOR IS A MUST!

THE OLD HYMNS, THE NEW SONGS, SHOULD SPEAK OF GOD'S
GRACE,
YOU SEE WE ARE TRYING TO RUN THIS CHRISTIAN RACE.

AUGUST 13, 2011

Inspiration

DID YOU LIKE THE PASTOR'S SERMON OF THE DAY?
TELL HIM, LET HIM KNOW IT, HE'S HELPING YOU IN A BIG WAY.

THE INSPIRATION OF KNOWING A PRAYING PREACHER,
WILL DO GOOD FOR THE CONGREGATION KNOWING HE IS OUR
SPIRITUAL TEACHER.

LISTEN, LEARN, PICK UP ON WHAT HE HAS TO SAY,
FOLLOW THE BIBLICAL TEXT AS HE GIVES YOU FOR THE DAY.

DON'T TAKE THE SERMON AND KEEP IT TO YOURSELF,
GO OUT AND SHARE IT WITH SOMEONE ELSE.

THE PASTOR ALWAYS TALK ABOUT GOD'S LOVE, AND HIS ALL TIME
GLORY,
WHY WOULDN'T YOU WANT TO HEAR ABOUT
GOD'S TEACHING STORIES.

WE CAN'T GET TO HEAVEN ON A WING AND PRAYER,
YOU'VE GOT TO KNOW GOD'S WORD TO GET YOU THERE.

WHEN YOU COME TO CHURCH, ENTER WITH THANKSGIVING,
COME TO HEAR THE WORD WITH A SMILE,
AN OPEN HEART, FOR GOD'S
WORD IS YOUR EVERYDAY LIVING.

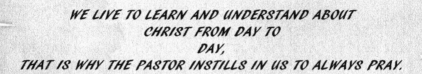

WE LIVE TO LEARN AND UNDERSTAND ABOUT
CHRIST FROM DAY TO
DAY,
THAT IS WHY THE PASTOR INSTILLS IN US TO ALWAYS PRAY.

IT'S GOOD TO KNOW THAT YOU HAVE A GOOD TEACHER.
IT'S NOT ABOUT HIS TITLE, THAT HE IS A PREACHER.

Bless The Children

LORD BLESS THE CHILDREN OF TODAY,
THEY NEED YOUR SPIRITUAL GUIDANCE IN A BIG WAY.

THEY ARE LOSING TOUCH OF WHO THEY ARE,
THEY ARE TAKING LIFE FOR GRANTED, AND HAVE
GONE A BIT TOO FAR

WHERE IS THE RESPECT AND LOVE FOR EACH OTHER TODAY,
HAVEN'T THEY BEEN TAUGHT BY THEIR PARENTS TO PRAY.

DO THEY KNOW THAT KILLING AND DRUGS IS NOT
THE ANSWER HERE,
DO THEY KNOW BY COMING TO THE LORD WILL
SOLVE THEIR FEAR.

WHY DON'T THE PARENTS HAVE THE UPPER
HAND IN THEIR CHILDS
LIFE,
DO THEY KNOW JESUS THEMSELVES, OR DO THEY NOT
WANT TO MAKE
A SACRIFICE.

WHEN A CHILD IS TAUGHT ABOUT GOD AT AN EARLY AGE,
THEY DON'T FORGET ABOUT THEIR ROOTS,
AND SOME TEND NOT TO
GO ASTRAY.

TALK TO YOUR CHILD AND LET THEM HEAR WHAT
YOU NEED TO SAY,
IT CAN HELP THEM TO GROW, AND HELP THEM ALONG THE WAY.

KNOWING THAT YOU PUT SOME KNOWLEDGE
INTO THEIR INQUISITIVE
MIND,
KNOWING THAT YOU PUT GOD FIRST WILL STAND
THE LENGTH OF
TIME.

LORD PLEASE BLESS THE CHILDREN FOR THEY ARE THE GROWING
ADULTS OF TODAY,
PLEASE INSTILL IN THEIR HEARTS AND MINDS,
THAT IT'S YOUR WAY OR NO WAY!

FOR EMANI

For Emani

EMANI, GRANNY FORGETS AT CERTAIN TIMES,
THOSE SPECIAL THINGS THAT I SHOULD KEEP IN MIND.

I FORGET BIRTHDAYS, APPOINTMENTS, AND A EGG
LEFT ON THE STOVE,
THAT'S SOME OF THE THINGS WE GRANNIES FORGET,
WHEN WE GET
OLD.

SOMETIMES I HAVE CALLED PEOPLE BY THE WRONG NAME,
THEIR FACES I DON'T FORGET, FOR WE ARE NOT ALL THE SAME.

AT TIMES I FORGET WHERE I PUT THE CAR KEYS,
AFTER I LOOK LONG ENOUGH, IN MY PURSE THEY WOULD BE.

EMANI ONE THING SPECIAL, I LOVE YOU AND THAT I WILL NEVER
FORGET.
ALLAH PUT YOU IN MY LIFE, AND YOU ARE THE BEST!

THE FIRST TIME I HELD YOU, THE BEAUTIFUL CHILD YOU ARE,
I PRAYED ALLAH WILL KEEP YOU FROM ALL DANGER AND HARM.

ALLAH WILL SHOW YOU, HE NEVER FORGETS!
WHEN YOU BECOME A GRANNY, THE STAGE IS SET.

LOVE YOU,
GRANNY TAYLOR

11-12-2009

Our children

Lord cover your children's mind with your perfect light.

Never let anyone harm them with the darkness of the night.

Keep these demonstrations which gives them something to think about.

Whatever it takes to show your love to them,

Let them give back, without doubt.

Notice To Parents

WHY LET YOUR CHILDREN LEARN TO GET HIGH ON DRUGS,
DO YOU KNOW IT'S NOT RIGHT TO THE LORD ABOVE!

CAN'T YOU LET THEM GET HIGH ON THE WORD OF JESUS CHRIST.
IT WILL TEACH THEM TO LOVE ONE ANOTHER, IT WILL TEACH THEM
WHAT IS RIGHT.

THEY NEED TO SURVIVE IN THIS SIN SICK WORLD, DRUGS WILL ONLY
KILL, AND KEEP THEIR HEADS IN A SWIRL.

THE WORD WILL TEACH THEM HOW TO GET TO HEAVEN, AND SHOW
THAT GOD REALLY CARES,
GOD WILL NOT PUT MORE ON THEM THAN THEY CAN BEAR.

LEAD THEM TO THE HEAVENLY FATHER, SO THEY CAN STOP.
DON'T YOU WANT YOUR LOVE ONE OFF DRUGS?
DON'T YOU WANT THEM ON TOP?

Meeting My Kinfolks

ONE DAY I'M GOING TO MEET MY KINFOLKS WAY UP THERE,
I'M GONNA SING AND SHOUT HALLELUJAH WITHOUT A CARE.

I'M GONNA HUG AND KISS EACH AND EVERYONE,
AND I WILL THANK GOD FOR ALL HE HAS DONE.

I WANT TO HAVE A FAMILY REUNION RIGHT ON
THE STREETS OF GOLD,
AND LISTEN TO ALL THE STORIES, I KNOW THERE'S
SOME GOOD ONES
TO BE TOLD.

I CAN'T WAIT TO EXPERIENCE GOD'S AMAZING GRACE,
WHEN I GET TO SEE HIM FACE TO FACE.

OH! WHEN GOD CALL ME TO HIM, AND TELLS ME WHAT TO DO,
I WILL FEEL HIS LOVE, BECAUSE I WILL BE BRAND NEW.

I'M GONNA BE WITH MY KINFOLKS, AND THERE'S NO SUCH THING AS
RACE OR COLOR HERE.
WE WILL ALL BE TREATED AS ONE WITH LOVE AND RESPECT,
WE'LL NEVER HAVE A THING TO FEAR.

The Aging Years

ONE DAY YOU WILL GROW OLDER, LIKE ALL OF US HAVE TO DO
YOU WOMEN CAN NO LONGER WEAR THAT DRESS SIZE TWO.

AND MEN THAT HAIR THAT USE TO BE AN AFRO!
IT WILL SHRINK AND SHRINK UNTIL THERE IS NO MORE.

SOME OF US WILL HAVE TO WEAR GLASSES,
OR WALK WITH A CANE,
BUT DON'T GET UPSET, FOR THERE'S NO ONE TO BLAME.

SOME HAVE AGED TO BE CALLED A SENIOR CITIZEN NOW,
BUT ONE GOOD THING ABOUT THIS, YOU CAN NOW GET YOUR
DISCOUNT DOWN.

YOU KNEW THAT THOSE GOOD OLD DAYS HAD TO
COME TO AN END.
BUT BY THE GRACE OF GOD HE HAS SUSTAINED YOU, AND HE'S
BEEN YOUR FAITHFUL FRIEND.

THE OTHER THING ABOUT GETTING OLDER,
JUST LOOK AROUND!
YOU CAN SEE YOUR KIDS MARRIED, GROWN,
AND NOW HAVE KIDS
OF THEIR OWN,
HOW GREAT IT IS TO BABYSIT YOUR GRANDKIDS FOR A LITTLE
WHILE, BUT WHEN YOU GET TIRED, YOU CAN CALL THEIR PARENTS,
KISS THEM, TELL THEM YOU LOVE THEM
AND SEND THEM HOME WITH A SMILE.

NOW IN THE QUIETNESS OF YOUR HOME YOU SIT BACK IN YOUR
FAVORITE CHAIR,
PICK UP THE GOOD BOOK, READ GOD'S WORD WITH
OUT ANY CARE.

IF YOU LOVE GOD AND YOU KNOW HIM PRAISE HIS HOLY NAME!
OUR AGE IS NOTHING BUT A NUMBER,
AND OUR LIVES WILL NEVER
BE THE SAME.

ONE TRUTH IS: ALL THESE YEARS GOD DIDN'T GIVE YOU THIS
KNOWLEDGE TO KEEP IT TO YOURSELF,
HE EXPECTS YOU TO SHARE THE JOY OF KNOWING HIM WITH
SOMEONE ELSE

IF YOU'RE SIXTY OR BLESSED TO BE A HUNDRED AND TWO
REMEMBER ALWAYS TRUST IN GOD, AND HE'LL TAKE CARE OF YOU.

OCTOBER 11, 2011

Friends And Family Day

A

FAMILY AND FRIENDS WE NEED YOU AROUND US,
WHEN PRAISING THE LORD TOGETHER,
THINK OF THE LIVES WE CAN
TOUCH.

CELEBRATION OF THE LOVE ONES WHO HAVE COME AND GONE,
GENERATION AFTER GENERATION, FAMILY AND FRIENDS LIVE ON.

WE DO NOT NEED A SPECIAL OCCASION BECAUSE IT'S ALWAYS A
FAMILY AFFAIR.
IT BRINGING OUR FRIENDS TOGETHER WITH US,
WE JUST WANT TO SHOW YOU WE CARE.

AUNT SUSIE, UNCLE WILL, WHERE HAVE YOU BEEN?
GOOD TO SEE YOU AT CHURCH TODAY,
DON'T MAKE THIS YOUR END.

LITTLE SHELLY, AND BILLY, THEY HAD SABBATH SCHOOL THIS
MORNING! YOU'RE WELCOME TO COME BACK,
YOU MIGHT THINK ABOUT
JOINING.

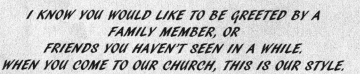

*I KNOW YOU WOULD LIKE TO BE GREETED BY A
FAMILY MEMBER, OR
FRIENDS YOU HAVEN'T SEEN IN A WHILE.
WHEN YOU COME TO OUR CHURCH, THIS IS OUR STYLE.*

*I KNOW THE PASTOR WOULD LOVE TO SEE YOUR SMILING FACE,
WELCOME FRIENDS AND FAMILY!
GOD'S PRESENCE IS IN THIS PLACE.*

Living Together

WHY CAN'T WE LIVE TOGETHER IN HARMONY,
THIS IS WHAT THE LORD INTENDED FOR YOU AND ME,

I'M SO TIRED OF SEEING ALL THE WRONG IN THIS WORLD TODAY,
IF WE WOULD JUST GIVE UP THE VIOLENCE, THROW DOWN OUR
WEAPONS, COME TOGETHER AND PRAY.

PRAYER CHANGES THINGS AND SHOWS YOU HOW TO LOVE YOUR
SISTERS AND BROTHERS,
IT SHOWS YOU HOW TO BE MORE RESPECTFUL TO YOUR FATHERS AND
MOTHERS.

IF THE TREND WENT ON LIKE THIS FROM GENERATION TO
GENERATION,
THE DEVIL WOULD NOT HAVE BEEN ABLE TO
ENTER IN OUR LIFE OF
PREPARATION.

WE ALL COULD HAVE LIVED WHEN JESUS
COMES BACK THE SECOND
TIME AROUND,
BUT SOME OF OUR SINFUL SOULS ARE FILLED WITH HATE,
AND THEY WILL NOT BE HEAVEN BOUND.

SOME DO NOT RESPECT GOD AS OUR MAKER AND SAVIOUR,
THEY WILL GO IN THE FIRE, BECAUSE OF THEIR BEHAVIOR.

IT'S NOT TO LATE TO TURN YOUR LIFE AROUND,
PRAY AND ASK FOR FORGIVENESS, COME TO JESUS RIGHT NOW!

IT'S SAD TO KNOW SOME WILL NEVER SEE YOUR FAMILY AGAIN,
IT'S SAD TO KNOW YOU WANT TO CONTINUE TO LIVE IN SIN.

Marriage

MARRIAGE IS A SACRED VOW THAT IS SHARED BY TWO,
SOME MEN ARE SO NAIVE, THAT THEY DON'T
KNOW WHAT TO DO.

ONCE THEY SAY I DO, AND SOME SAY I WILL,
OTHERS BEGAN TO SHOW THAT IT WAS NO BIG DEAL.

THE SECOND DAY OF MARRIAGE, THEY THINK IT'S LIKE A YEAR,
THEY SIT BACK ON THEIR LAZY BUTTS, WITH T.V. AND A BEER,

I LIKE TO KNOW WHY SOME ENTER INTO MARRIAGE IN THE FIRST
PLACE,
WHEN THEY CAN'T EVEN SIT AND TALK TO THEIR SPOUSE FACE TO
FACE.

WHEN IT COMES TO THE POINT WHEN THE SPOUSE CAN'T TAKE IT
ANYMORE,
DIVORCE IS CONSIDERED, AND THEY BOTH ARE OUT THE DOOR.

I PRAY GOD WILL STAY IN MY RELATIONSHIP,
I ENTERED INTO THIS MARRIAGE FOR THE LONG, LONG TRIP.

MARRIAGES ARE ABOUT LOVE, AND IT NEEDS TO WORK OUT,
IT TOOK TWO TO GET MARRIED AND IT'S NOT
ABOUT ONE SPOUSE.

PUTTING GOD FIRST, AND WORKING IT OUT DAY BY DAY,
THIS IS THE ONLY SOLUTION IN ANY MARRIAGE,
WITH GOD, THERE IS NO OTHER WAY!

Trust In Marriage

WHEN YOU ARE COMMITTED TO A RELATIONSHIP,
AND YOUR SPOUSE
DO NOT PUT GOD FIRST IN THEIR LIFE,
YOU KNOW THIS IS NOT THE WAY TO LIVE,
AND YOU KNOW THIS IS NOT
RIGHT.

YOU CAN'T SEEM TO GET ALONG AND SHARE THE SAME VIEW,
THAT'S BECAUSE YOU ARE NOT AS ONE, BUT A SEPARATED TWO.

THE FIRST THING TO DO IS PRAY, AND NEVER GIVE UP!
YOU MAY FEEL THAT YOUR DAYS ARE ALWAYS FILLED WITH A FULL
CUP.

I KNOW MARRIAGE IS A BIG TASK IN UNDERSTANDING ONE ANOTHER,
WITHOUT GOD AND LOVE IN YOUR LIFE, YOUR MARRIAGE CAN GO
UNDER.

BLESSINGS WILL NOT COME TO TWO WHERE ONE
DON'T KNOW WHAT
GOD CAN DO.
READING GOD'S WORD IS THE BEST TOOL.

IT'S NOT GOOD TO ALWAYS THINK OF ONESELF,
IT'S ABOUT KNOWING GOD, AND ASKING FOR HELP.

THE WAY YOU TAKE TIME OUT FOR OTHERS AND NEGLECT YOUR
HOME,
YOU ACT LIKE YOU'RE A BIG KING SITTING ON A THRONE.

I'M A HUMAN BEING, AND WE NEED TO TREAT
EACH OTHER AS SUCH,
PUTTING GOD IN YOUR MARRIAGE IS TRULY A MUST.

YOU ARE NOT MY GOD, AND YOU DO NOT SIT ON A THRONE,
IF YOU DON'T CHANGE YOUR WAY OF LIFE,
YOU WILL BE ALL ALONE.

(12/31/2011)

Happiness

HAPPINESS SEEMS LIKE A THING OF THE PASS,
YOU THINK IT'S SUPPOSE TO LAST AND LAST.

I'M HEAR TO TELL YOU, AND LET YOU KNOW,
IT TAKE A LOTS TO LET LOVE GROW.

WHEN YOU TRY TO DO THE BEST YOU CAN,
THE DEVIL IS BUSY ON EVERY HAND.

YOU TAKE A LOTS OFF THE PEOPLE YOU LOVE,
ITS LIKE TRYING TO FIT YOUR HANDS IN A TIGHT GLOVE.

DOES HAPPINESS COME IN A DOOGY BAG,
SHOULD I WAG MY TAIL NOW, AND BE GLAD.

SOMETIMES I PRAY AND THANK THE LORD UP ABOVE,
THAT HE GAVE ME STRENGTH, HIS HAPPINESS AND HIS LOVE.

WITHOUT HIM YOU CAN'T FIND TOTAL
HAPPINESS HEAR ON EARTH,
SO I TAKE WHAT I CAN UNTIL GOD GIVES ME A NEW BIRTH.

A NEW BIRTH IS GOD'S KINGDOM ABOVE,
THERE I KNOW I'LL FIND NOTHING BUT HAPPINESS AND LOVE.

A Dream Of Time

TIME IS LOVE, FOR IT IS TIMELESS.

AS MANY GRAINS OF SAND ON THE DESERT FLOOR,
TO COUNT THEM ALL I LOVE YOU MORE.

AS BRILLIANT AS THE SUN WE DO ADORE,
AS VAST AS THE HEAVENS FROM SHORE TO SHORE.

WE SHARE GOD'S LOVE WHICH IS TIMELESS, AND EVERLASTING AS
OUR FAITH.

UNTO EACH OTHER WE SHALL ENDURE,
TO LOVE, TO GROW TO BE SECURE.

TIMELESS, TIMELESS, HIS WILL BE DONE.

There Is No Substitute

THERE IS NO SUBSTITUTE FOR GOD'S PRAISE,
TRY HIM FOR YOURSELF, AND YOU WILL BE AMAZED.

LIFT YOUR VOICE TO HEAVEN, AND SING PRAISES TO HIM,
HE'S OUR STRENGTH AND LIGHT, WHEN THINGS SEEM TO BE DIM.

WHEN YOU NEED THE SAVIOR, WHEN IT A BAD DAY,
KNEEL DOWN ON YOUR KNEES, TELL HIM ABOUT
IT AND JUST PRAY.

THERE IS NOTHING YOU CAN'T ASK FOR, AND HE CAN'T DO,
HE'S A MIRACLE WORKER, AND HE'LL WORK IT OUT FOR YOU.

YOU CAN'T FIND, A BETTER FRIEND THAN HIM,
SEE IF YOUR SO CALLED FRIEND WILL STEP OUT ON A LIMB.

YOU CAN EVEN ASK YOUR FAMILY FOR HELP, AND SEE WHAT THEY
WILL DO,
ASKING THEM FOR HELP IS LIKE BITING OFF MORE THAN YOU CAN
CHEW.

WHEN YOU REALIZE THERE IS NO ONE ELSE YOU CAN DEPEND ON
FOR GUIDANCE AND HELP.
YOU SHOULD KNOW NOW WHAT DIRECTION TO GO IN,
AND MAKE SURE THAT IT'S THE RIGHT STEP.

Growing Old

THAT LITTLE OLD PERSON THAT YOU'RE TALKING ABOUT,
THIS COULD BE A MOTHER, A FATHER, OR SOMEONE'S SPOUSE.

THESE ARE PEOPLE YOU SOMETIMES TRY TO AVOID,
YOU DON'T KNOW THIS, BUT THEY ARE CLOSE TO THE LORD.

THEY ARE ALWAYS PRAYING FOR YOU AND FOR ME,
FOR ONE DAY THEY ALL WILL BE FREE.

WITH THEIR EXPERIENCE OF A LIFETIME WE WISH WE HAD,
THEY HAVE SEEN MORE OF LIFE, THE GOOD AND THE BAD.

THEY CAN TELL YOU SOME STORIES, EVEN OF THE SLAVERY DAY,
BUT LIVING THROUGH THIS, GOD WAS WITH THEM
EVERY STEP OF THE WAY.

THE RESPECT THEY DESERVE, AND IT SHOULD BE GIVEN.
ALL PRAISES TO THEM FOR THE LONG LIFE THEY ARE LIVING.

ONE DAY WE MAY GROW OLD, I PRAY WITH GOD IN OUR LIVES,
ALSO WITH FAMILY AND FRIENDS, STILL BY OUR SIDES.

WHEN YOU SEE A OLD PERSON AND THEY NEED SOME HELP,
REMEMBER YOU MAY REACH THIS LEVEL YOURSELF.

NOW DAYS SOME YOUTH DON'T GET TO BE OLD,
SOME LIVE TO FAST, AND SOME ARE TO BOLD.

GROWING OLD IS A BLESSING WITHIN ITSELF,
IT'S A BLESSING THAT THE HEAVENLY FATHER DEALT.

What Do I Owe God

I OWE GOD THE RESPECT TO LOVE OTHERS AS I DO MYSELF,
TO READ HIS WORD, UNDERSTAND, AND FEEL AS HE FELT.

I'M TO TELL OTHERS ABOUT HIS UNDYING LOVE,
HOW TO REACH THE
HIGHEST POTENTIAL TO GET TO HEAVEN ABOVE.

I OWE GOD TO STAY AWAY FROM THINGS THAT ARE NOT RIGHT.
TO STAY FAR FROM THE DEVILISH THINGS,
TO BE STRONG AND FIGHT.

IT'S MY DUTY TO TELL AND TEACH THE CHILDREN OF TODAY,
THERE IS A GOD WHO LOVES THEM, AND PROTECT THEM,
BUT THEY
MUST LEARN HOW TO PRAY.

I MUST TELL THEM TO LEARN ABOUT GOD, AND IT'S GOD CHURCH THEY
MUST ATTEND,
WITH THEM LEARNING FROM THE STREETS WILL
ONLY LEARN ABOUT SIN.

I OWE MY LOVE FOR YOU LORD, FOR SENDING ME
A HUSBAND I PRAY
FOR LIFE.
AS LONG AS HE SERVES YOU LORD AND RESPECT ME, I WILL ALWAYS
BE HIS WIFE.

LORD GOD YOU HAVE PLACED MY FAMILY, CHILDREN AND
GRANDCHILDREN TO BE WITH ME DOWN HERE ON EARTH,
I TELL THEM ABOUT YOUR GOODNESS, YOUR LOVE,
AND WHAT IT IS
WORTH.

GOD I OWE YOU MY LIFE, AND I THANK YOU FOR ALL
YOU HAVE DONE
FOR ME,
IF NOT FOR YOUR LOVE AND MERCY, I DON'T KNOW
WHERE MY LIFE
WOULD BE.

Where There Is

WHERE THERE IS A MAN AND A WOMAN,
THERE SHOULD BE LOVE.

WHERE THERE IS CHILDREN,
YOU ARE NEVER ALONE.

WHERE THERE IS FAMILY, DON'T KEEP THEM TO YOURSELF,
THESE ARE PEOPLE IN YOUR LIFE THAT MAY NEED HELP.

WHERE THERE IS A CHURCH THAT YOU ATTEND,
YOU CAN ALWAYS FIND A CHRISTIAN FRIEND.

WHERE THERE IS TROUBLE YOU TURN FROM IT!
TO STAY AROUND YOU ARE TAKING A BIG RISK.

WHERE THERE IS DOUBT, PRAY FOR GOODNESS SAKE,
MAKING THE WRONG DECISION CAN BE TOO LATE.

WHERE YOU FEEL SATAN IS TRYING TO DESTROY YOUR LIFE,
KNEEL TO THE HEAVENLY FATHER TO PRAY,
HE'LL MAKE EVERYTHING
ALRIGHT.

(12/31/2011)

Life

I KNOW LIFE HAVEN'T BEEN SO SMOOTH,
BUT THINGS ARE GOING TO WORK OUT FOR YOU.

YOU SAY THAT THE ROAD IS REALLY ROUGH FOR YOU
BUT GOD IS GOING TO SEE YOU THROUGH.

YOU EVEN SAY "WHY ME", WHAT DID I DO WRONG,
LET ME TELL YOU, THAT'S A SAD OLD SONG.

LIFE IS WHAT YOU PUT IN TO IT!,
SOMETIMES IT HURTS, BUT YOU HAVE TO COMMIT.

READ YOUR BIBLE FOR YOUR DAILY BREAD,
GOD WILL GIVE YOU STRENGTH,
ISN'T THAT "WHAT HE SAID."

TAKE THE WORDS OF THE LORD, TO LIVE YOUR LIFE,
IT WILL HELP YOU TO GROW IN THIS WORLD OF,
EVERY DAY STRIFE.

Sisters In Christ

SISTERS IN CHRIST SHOULD BE AS ONE,
PRAISING GOD IN THE HIGHEST, TILL HIS WILL BE DONE.

SHARING THE JOY IN SPIRIT, AND IN TRUTH,
WE SHOULD BE TELLING OUR FAMILIES ABOUT
OUR CHURCH ROOTS.

WE AS FEMALES CAN BE SISTERS IN CHRIST,
IF WE JUST KEEP OUR PERSPECTIVES RIGHT.

NOT ONE OR TWO CAN LEAD THE WAY,
WE ALL NEED TO GET TOGETHER AND PRAY.

SISTERS MEAN A LOTS TODAY,
WE STAND IN THE LIGHT IN SO MANY WAYS.

IT DOESN'T MATTER HOW EDUCATED YOU ARE,
OR WHERE YOU HAVE
BEEN.
GOD LOOKS AT OUR HEARTS, DEEP WITHIN.

ALL OF US HAVE SOME TALENTS TO SHARE,
SO COME JOIN WITH THE SISTERS, WE DO CARE!

LET US JOIN HANDS, PRAY WITH THE SISTERS IN CHRIST,
WITH PRAYERS GOING UP, GOD WILL MAKE THINGS ALRIGHT.

My Last

LORD I'VE ALWAYS TRIED TO DO WHAT IS RIGHT,
I'M SOMETIMES MISTREATED DAY AND NIGHT.

LORD WHAT WAS I PUT ON THIS EARTH TO DO,
TO BE LIED ON, AND TALKED ABOUT LIKE THEY DID TO YOU.

I'M BEING HURT BY PEOPLE WHO SAY THEY LOVE ME,
I CAN IMAGINE HOW IT FELT WHEN YOU WHERE FINALLY FREE.

LORD YOU ARE SO MUCH STRONGER THAN ME,
I AM WEAK AND I'M TIRED, AND IT'S YOU THAT I NEED.

WHAT AM I TO DO WHEN THE BURDEN IS TOO DEEP,
WHEN I LAY AWAKE AT NIGHT AND I CAN'T SLEEP.

THINGS HAVE GOTTEN SO BAD HERE ON EARTH,
LIVING HERE QUESTIONS WHAT IS MY LIFE WORTH?

EVILNESS, NO LOVE SHOWN, AND HATRED IN ONES HOUSE,
EVERYONE SAY THEY LOVE YOU LORD, SO WHAT IS THIS ABOUT?

I TRY TO SERVE YOU LORD, AND EVEN GO TO CHURCH,
I COME HOME TO A FEELING OF NOT WORTH.

LORD WILL YOU TAKE ME TO YOUR HOME WHERE
THERE IS SO MUCH
LOVE AND PEACE,
I KNOW I'M GONNA SHOUT FOR JOY, PRAISE YOUR NAME WITH A
GREAT SIGH OF RELIEF.

I KNOW LORD BY READING YOUR WORD THERE
IS NO GREATER JOY
THAN BEING IN HEAVEN WITH YOU.
YOU KNOW HOW TO TREAT YOUR CHILDREN RIGHT,
AND ONLY YOU
KNOW WHAT TO DO!

I'M GONNA WAIT LORD TO YOU BRING YOUR CHILD HOME,
WHERE I WILL BE LOVED, AND NEVER FEEL ALONE.

What If

I

WHAT WOULD IT BE LIKE IF THERE WAS NO DAY?
WHAT WOULD IT BE LIKE IF THERE WAS NO LIGHT?
IT WOULD BE LIKE NOT HAVING JESUS IN YOUR LIFE.

WHAT WOULD IT BE LIKE IF THERE WAS NO RAIN TO MAKE THE
FLOWERS BLOOM, OR MAKE THE FRUIT GROW,
IT WOULD BE LIKE NOT HAVING JESUS AROUND,
AND I REALLY DON'T
WANT TO KNOW.

WHAT WOULD IT BE LIKE IF THERE WAS NO CHURCH, WHERE WE CAN
GO TO WORSHIP AND PRAY.
IT WOULD BE LIKE NOT HAVING JESUS AROUND
AND HEARING WHAT HE
HAS TO SAY.

WHAT WOULD IT BE LIKE IF THERE WAS NO LOVE IN THE WORLD
TODAY,
IT WOULD BE LIKE A SIN SICK WORLD FULL OF HATRED TO STAY.
IT WOULD BE NOT LIKE HAVING JESUS IN OUR LIFE AND THAT'S TO
MUCH TO FIGHT.

I'M GLAD I DON'T HAVE TO FACE THE REALITY THAT JESUS IS NOT IN
MY
LIFE, AND WONDER IF,
FOR YOU DON'T WANT TO FALL PREY TO THE DEVIL
AND TAKE THAT
HORRIBLE TRIP.

A Forgetful Day

OH! WHAT DID I FORGET TODAY,
AS I HURRIEDLY ALONG MY WAY.

DID I FORGET TO LOCK THE DOOR,
WHEN I WENT TO THE GROCERY STORE.

DID I FORGET TO TURN ON THE FISH TANK,
OR DID I FORGET TO PAY THE BANK.

MY MIND IS SO BUSY AT TIMES,
I CAN'T SEEM TO THINK THE SIZE OF A DIME.

DID I FORGET TO TURN OFF THE COFFEE POT,
OR DID I CHECK TO SEE IF THE BACK DOOR WAS LOCKED.

I KNOW THAT I AM GETTING OLD,
"IT'S JUST IN YOUR MIND," I AM TOLD.

I MAY HAVE NEEDED ANOTHER CUP OF COFFEE TO WAKE UP,
MY SLEEP LAST NIGHT WAS A LITTLE DISRUPT.

NOW I REMEMBERED AS I ROSE ON THIS BLESSED DAY,
THE MOST IMPORTANT THING IS, I FORGOT TO PRAY.

1-18-2009

Black History

IN OUR BLACK HISTORY, THERE IS A LOT OF AMERICAN GREATS.
YEARS OF SERVICE TO THIS COUNTRY, THAT'S WHY WE CELEBRATE.

THE MONTH OF FEBRUARY WE CELEBRATE BLACK PRIDE.
WE SALUTE BLACK WOMEN AND BLACK MEN WHO PUT THEIR
DIFFERENCES ASIDE.

THE COLOR OF THEIR SKIN DIDN'T STOP THEM AT ALL.
WE PRAISE THEM AND COMMEND THEM
THEY WASN'T BREAKING A
LAW.

WE HAVE COME A LONG WAY FROM SLAVERY DAYS'
WE CAN SPEAK UP AND SPEAK OUT,
THEY LISTEN TO WHAT WE HAVE TO SAY.

THERE WERE GREAT CIVIL RIGHT ACTIVIST LIKE MEDGER EVERS,
MARTIN LUTHER KING, AND STOKELY CARMICHEAL TOO,
LEADERS LIKE WASHINGTON CARVER, W.E.B. DUBOIS, MALCOLM X,
MARCUS GARVEY, WHITNEY YOUNG, JUST TO NAME A FEW.

SPORTS WAS A BIG THING DOWN IN HISTORY FOR SURE.
HEARTACHES AND PAIN WHICH ALL HAD TO INDURE.

GEORGE DIXON IN 1870 WAS THE FIRST BLACK TO FIGHT AND WIN,
MIKE FUSUN, JOE LOUIS, THEN MUHAMMED ALI, STEPPED IN.

BASEBALL GREAT, JOSH GIBSON BORN 1911 FIRST NEGRO LEAGUE
PLAYER,
HANK ARON, JACKIE ROBINSON, WILLIE MAYS, ALL CAME LATER.

WE HAVE SO MANY SPORTS PEOPLE TODAY TO NAME.
GOLF, FOOTBALL, TRACK, BLACKS ARE IN THE HALL OF FAME.

THE FIRST BLACK FEMALE ASTRONAUT MAY JEMISON WAS A
PHYSICIAN ALSO.
BLACK WOMEN RUN FOR OFFICES, AND ARE ELECTED
AT THE POLL.

GREAT BLACK WOMEN OF GOVERNMENT, MUSIC SPORTS, LEADERS,
AND ACTIVIST.
HARRIET TUBMAN, JOSEPHINE BAKER, LENA HORNE, MARY BETHUNE,
AND BESSIE SMITH.

MANY, MANY BLACKS HAVE PAVED THE WAY.
GOD BLESS THEM ALL FOR A BETTER DAY.

Health And Fitness

GOD CHOSE THE FOODS WE MUST EAT,
HE HAS NAMED THEM, PREPARED THEM, AND IT'S FOR OUR TREAT.

HE ONLY WANTS TO PROTECT THE TEMPLE, "OUR BODIES"
THIS BELONGS TO HIM.
IN ACCORDANCE WITH GOD'S LAW, ALL SHOULD BE FIT AND TRIM.

THE LIFE GIVEN FLUID OF THE BODY IS WATER, WHICH SHOULD BE
FREE FOR ALL,
DRINKING BEER AND LIQUOR IS BAD ALCOHOL.

EATING THE PROPER FRUITS AND FOODS, GOD'S WRITTEN WORD
TELLS US WHAT TO EAT.
NO SWINE, NO PORK, THE PIG IS THE WORST POISON MEAT.

LOTS OF FRUITS, NUTS, AND VEGETABLES IS OUR MOST HEALTHY
SOURCE OF EATING,
FOLLOWING GOD'S HEALTH REGIMEN WILL HELP THE BODY FROM
TAKING A BEATING.

DOING SOME SORT OF EXERCISE WILL HELP OUR HEARTS,
MIND, AND
LIMBS TO OPERATE A LITTLE BETTER.
STOP THE CHATTER, DO WHAT MATTERS, AND WE'LL GET THERE
TOGETHER.

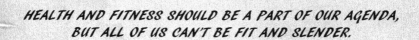

HEALTH AND FITNESS SHOULD BE A PART OF OUR AGENDA,
BUT ALL OF US CAN'T BE FIT AND SLENDER.

GOD MADE ALL OF US, BUT WHAT WE DO TO OUR BODIES,
WE DO ON OUR OWN,
BUT THAT DAY WHEN WE MEET OUR MAKER,
WE WILL SAT HEALTHY AT HIS THRONE.

A New Year

I

A YEAR IS COMING IN,
WE NEED YOU JESUS MORE THAN EVER TO BE OUR FRIEND.

THINGS HAVE NOT CHANGED AT ALL IN THE YEAR PASS,
I DON'T BELIEVE LORD THAT WE'VE DONE OUR BEST.

PRAYERS ARE THAT YOU'RE SOON TO COME,
OUR LIVES ARE NOT RIGHT, AND YOUR WILL BE DONE.

TRYING TO PLEASE IN A WORLD WHERE THERE IS LESS LOVE,
IT'S NOT THE LIFE THAT YOU BROUGHT US FROM.

LORD! THIS WORLD WILL NEVER BE RIGHT'
UNLESS YOU COME AND TAKE US TO THE LIGHT.

FAMILIES AND CHILDREN ARE FALLING APART,
MOST OF THEIR LIVES ARE IN THE DARK.

SOME DON'T EVEN RESPECT YOU!
I KNOW THERE IS VERY LITTLE WE CAN DO.

WE CAN ONLY PRAY FOR THOSE WHO ARE OUT OF TOUCH.
THEY NEED YOU IN THEIR LIFE, EVER SO MUCH.

TIMES ARE ROUGH, BUT WE SHOULD NEVER GIVE UP ON YOU!
LIVING WITHOUT YOU, WHAT ARE WE SUPPOSE TO DO?

EVEN SOMETIMES IN OUR HOMES, THERE IS NO PEACE,
KNOWING THE JOY THAT ONE DAY, YOU'RE GIVE US OUR RELIEF.

Christmas

CHRISTMAS IS THAT TIME OF YEAR,
WE CELEBRATE AND BE OF GOOD CHEER.

THERE IS NOTHING WRONG IN EXCHANGING A GIFT.
IT SHOWS WE CARE ABOUT YOU, THIS SHOULD GIVE YOU A LIFT.

CHILDREN EXPECT TO WAKE UP ON THIS DAY,
THEIR EYES FILLED WITH JOY, AND HOPING TO GET THAT SPECIAL TOY.

FRIENDS AND FAMILY MAY VISIT THAT DAY,
BRINGING A COVERED DISH, AND HOPE YOU GOT YOUR WISH.

WHAT WE SHOULD CELEBRATE IS THE DAY CHRIST WAS BORN,
NOT WORRYING ABOUT A SPECIAL TOY.

CHRIST IS THE GIFT OF LOVE, HE'S THE GIFT OF FAITH,
HE'S THE GIFT OF LIFE, AND HE'S THE GIFT OF GRACE.

NOW THINK OF WHY WE CELEBRATE THIS HOLIDAY SEASON,
THAT'S WHY CHRIST IS IN FRONT OF CHRISTMAS
TO COMPLETE THE
WORD FOR THE REASON.

THANK CHRIST FOR THE MANY BLESSINGS AND GIFTS
HE GIVES THIS
YEAR,
WHEN YOU DO THIS IT IS SPREADING LOVE AND GOOD CHEER.

Easter

EASTER, THE WORD MAN GAVE US TO CELEBRATE,
WHAT THEY USE IT FOR, IT'S ABOUT THE MONEY THEY MAKE.

THE ONLY THING EASTER IS SPELLED OUT BY LETTER IS:

E—EGG HUNT
A—AMUSEMENT
S—STYLISH CLOTHES
T—TULIPS
E—IMITATION
AND R—RACE

BUT WHAT GOD HAVE DONE FOR US IT'S NOT ABOUT EASTER
WHY WE CELEBRATE!

TELL OUR CHILDREN THE MEANING OF THE PASS OVER DAY,
JOIN TOGETHER WITH OUR FAMILIES, LET'S TALK ABOUT IT AND
PRAY.

TELL THEM THE TRUE MEANING OF JESUS CHRIST CRUCIFIXION,
AND HOW HE DIED TO SAVE US ALL OF OUR CONVICTION.

TELL HOW OUR JESUS AROSE FROM WHERE HE LAYED,
MOVED THE STONE FROM THE ENTRANCE AND THEN WALKED AWAY.

TELL HOW HE WALKED TO THE CITY OF GALILEE,
SO OUR SINFUL SOULS COULD BE SET FREE.

TELL HOW THE PEOPLE SHOUTED HE AROSE! HE AROSE! HE AROSE FROM THE GRAVE,
LET THE CHILDREN KNOW WHY WE SING THIS SONG TODAY.

CELEBRATE! CELEBRATE!, HAVE A HALLELUIAH GOOD TIME
BE REMINDED WHY WE CELEBRATE, IT'S ABOUT KEEPING CHRIST IN MIND.

Mother's Day

THIS IS A SPECIAL DAY
SPECIAL IN EVERY WAY.
THIS IS A DAY FOR ALL MOTHERS,
THIS DAY IS MOTHER'S DAY.

ONE MONTH OF EVERY YEAR IS PUT A SIDE TO SAY,
WE LOVE YOU MOM NOT ONLY IN MAY, BUT FOREVER, AND
EVER WE PRAY.

WE APPRECIATE YOU MOM, FOR ALL THAT YOU HAVE DONE,
YOU HAVE RAISED US TO BE A PRODUCTIVE DAUGHTER, AND
SON.

THAT CHILD THAT WAS TAUGHT RIGHT, BUT CHOSE TO GO
ASTRAY,
YOU SOMETIMES FIGHT A LOSING BATTLE,
BUT LET GOD HANDLE IT HIS WAY!

YOU STRONG WOMEN WHO GAVE US BIRTH, AND NEVER LEFT
OUR SIDE.
GOD BLESS AND KEEP EVERYONE ONE OF YOU, AND LET GOD
BE YOUR ONLY GUIDE.

FOR ALL THE MOTHERS WHO HAVE PASSED ON,
FOR EVERY MEMORY AND THOUGHT,
JUST THINK OF ALL THE CARE THEY GAVE YOU, AND ALL
THE JOY THEY BROUGHT.

WHEN ALL IS SAID AND DONE, THERE IS NO OTHER.
NO ONE IN THE WORLD, CAN REPLACE YOUR LOVING
MOTHER. (L. TAYLOR)

Father's Day

THIS IS A SPECIAL DAY, AND SPECIAL IN EVERY WAY,
THIS DAY IS FOR ALL FATHERS, THIS IS FATHER'S DAY!

ONE DAY OUT OF A MONTH, AND EVERY YEAR IS SET A SIDE TO SAY,
"DAD WE LOVE YOU! NOT ONLY TO TODAY, BUT
MORE THAN WORDS
CAN SAY".

WE APPRECIATE YOU, FOR ALL THAT YOU HAVE DONE,
YOU HAVE RAISED US TO BE A PRODUCTIVE DAUGHTER,
AND SON.

THAT CHILD THAT WAS RAISED RIGHT, BUT CHOSE TO GO ASTRAY,
YOU SOMETIMES FIGHT A LOSING BATTLE, BUT LET GOD HAVE HIS WAY.

YOU STRONG MEN WHO HAVE FOUGHT AND NEVER LEFT
OUR SIDE.
GOD BLESS AND KEEP YOU, AND LET GOD BE YOUR GUIDE.

Father's Day

FATHER DAY IS A DAY SET A SIDE,
IT'S FOR THE FATHERS TO LIFT THEIR HEADS WITH PRIDE.

A MAN FIRST WHO LOVES THE LORD, AND STAYS IN HIS
WORD,
THIS IS A MAN WHOM IS WELL DESERVED.

THIS MAN'S HOUSE IS A HOUSE OF LOVE,
THE WHOLE HOUSE KNOWS ABOUT GOD IN HEAVEN ABOVE.

HE SUPPORTS HIS FAMILY ONE HUNDRED PERCENT,
HE GOES TO WORK, PUT FOOD ON THE TABLE, AND PAYS THE
RENT.

HE HELPS HIS CHILDREN WITH PROBLEMS IN SCHOOL,
HE TEACHES THEM WELL ABOUT THE GOLDEN RULE.

EVERYONE AROUND HIM RESPECTS HIM AS A MAN,
GOD MADE HIM IN HIS IMAGE, AND THAT'S THE WAY IT
STANDS.

THE FAMILY GOING TO CHURCH TOGETHER,
AND GOING ON OUTINGS TOO.
THANK GOD FOR FATHERS LIKE THIS WHO KNOWS WHAT TO
DO.

WE SHOULD THINK OF OUR FATHERS IF THEY ARE
YOUNG, OLD, OR IF THEY HAVE PASSED ON,
GOD PUT THEM IN OUR LIVES A LONG TIME AGO.

SOME FATHERS WE THINK ARE NOT WORTHY AND NEVER
ATTEND TO OUR NEEDS,
WITHOUT THEM, THERE WOULD NOT HAVE BEEN A MALE OR
FEMALE SEED.

WE TAKE THE TIME TO PRAY FOR ALL THE FATHERS ALL
OVER THE WORLD,
THIS COMES FROM THE FAMILIES, YOUR SON, OR YOUR
GIRL.

A Thanksgiving Prayer

ON THIS DAY OF THANKSGIVING, LORD WE GIVE THANKS TO YOU!
THANKS FOR ALL THE WONDERFUL THINGS YOU DO.

IF IT WASN'T FOR YOUR GENEROSITY,
WHERE WOULD OUR FAMILIES AND OUR LOVED ONES BE.

YOU PUT FOOD ON OUR TABLES, AND CLOTHES ON OUR BACKS'
SHOES ON OUR FEET, AND A WARM PLACE TO SLEEP.

YOU'VE HEALED OUR BODIES, CLEANSED OUR MINDS,
AND MADE US STRONG.
WITHOUT YOU IN OUR LIVES, EVERYTHING WOULD GO WRONG.

WE SHOULD PRAISE YOUR NAME FOREVER MORE,
YOU HAVE OPENED UP OUR HEARTS, AND OPENED
SO MANY DOORS.

THE DOORS OF HAPPINESS, OR THE DOORS TO BE SAD,
WHATEVER GOD HAS TO OFFER US, WE SHOULD BE GLAD.

WHAT GOD DOES NO ONE CAN COMPARE,
HE DOESN'T PUT MORE ON US THAN WE CAN BARE.

911

ℐ

WHEN YOU MENTION THE NUMBER 911,
IT HAS A SPECIAL MEANING TO ME,
YOU THINK OF THE PEOPLE WHO DIED IN A TERRIBLE TRAGEDY.

THE PEOPLE WHO WENT ABOUT THEIR DAY AT WORK
TO TAKE CARE OF THEIR FAMILIES.
THEY NEVER THOUGHT THAT THIS DAY WOULD
END IN A TERRIBLE
FATALITY,

HOW CAN THESE PEOPLE TAKE THEIR LIVES, AND THE INNOCENT
LIVES OF OTHERS.
HOW CAN THEY CONFESS TO LOVING GOD, AND THEMSELVES,
THEN TAKE THE LIVES OF THEIR OWN BROTHERS.

THIS IS THE WORSE THING THAT HAVE HAPPENED TO US,
ON OUR OWN HOME GROUND,
TAKING THE LIVES OF SO MANY LOVED ONES,
HAVE BEEN A LET DOWN.

SEPTEMBER 11, 2001 IS A DAY WE WILL ALWAYS REGRET,
WE PRAY GOD WILL MAKE US STRONG, AND NOT DO WRONG,
FOR THIS IS A DAY WE NEVER FORGET.

GOD OPENED OUR EYES TO A DAY THAT WE TOOK FOR GRANTED,
THE BIBLE SPEAKS OF THE EVIL DOERS OF THIS WORLD WHO ARE,
MEAN, CRUEL, AND SATANIC.

IF WE WOULD STOP HATING ONE ANOTHER BECAUSE OF RACE,
RELIGION, OR JUST BEING POOR,
GOD WILL OPEN UP HIS HEART OF PROTECTION, THE KIND YOU'RE
LOOKING FOR.

THERE IS PROTECTION NOW WHEN GOD TOOK HIS CHILDREN HOME OF
THE 911 INCIDENT
GOD OPENED HIS OUT STRETCHED HANDS AND EXCEPTED THEM IN.

Commitment

IN THE YEARS BEHIND US, OUR LOVED ONES HAVE
COME AND GONE,
WE HAVE ANOTHER YEAR IN FRONT OF US, GOD EXPECTS US TO CARRY
ON.

WE'VE SEEN THE DEVIL BUSY IN OUR CHILDREN'S LIVES,
WE SEE OUR PEOPLE UNHAPPY, AS OUR RACE DIVIDES.

WE SEE OUR LEADERS FALL, DRUG DEALINGS AND THE KILLINGS,
WE NEED TO CHECK OURSELVES AND ASK, IF OUR LIFE IS FULFILLING.

SOME OF YOU ASK, "WHAT MUST I DO TO BE SAVED"?
READ YOUR BIBLE, TRUST IN GOD, AND MOST OF ALL PRAY.

HE WANTS US TO HELP OTHERS COME TO CHRIST
AND NOT THINKING ONLY OF OUR FEELINGS,
GOD EXPECTS US TO BE LEADERS, TO BE SINCERE AND WILLING.

Do You Want To Go To Heaven?

WHO WANT TO GO TO HEAVEN FOR GOODNESS SAKE,
WHO WANTS TO GO TO HEAVEN TO SEE THE PEARLY GATES?

WHO WANTS TO GO TO HEAVEN TO SEE THE STREETS OF GOLD,
IT'S TOLD IN THE BIBLE HOW BEAUTIFUL IT WILL UNFOLD.

WHO WANTS TO SEE THE MASTER FACE TO FACE,
WHO WANTS TO HERE HIM TELL YOU,
"YOU'VE BEEN SAVED BY GRACE"!.

WHO WANT TO HERE JESUS SAY, "YOU ARE HEALED"!,
AND TELL YOU NO MORE PROBLEMS WILL BE REVEALED.

WHO WANTS TO SEE YOUR FAMILY AND FRIENDS AGAIN,
WHO WANTS TO GO TO THAT HOLYLAND.

WHO WANTS TO SING IN THE HOLY CHOIR,
TO BE DRESSED IN THE GARMENTS OF WHITE ATTIRE.

WHO WANTS TO BE CLEANSED AND CLEAR OF MIND.
HAVE FAITH, PRAY, WAIT ON THE LORD TILL IT'S YOUR TIME.

Be Ready

YOU SEE THAT OUR TIME ON EARTH IS NEAR,
BE SAVED BY GRACE AND HAVE NO FEAR.

THE BIBLE TELLS WHEN, AND IT'S BEING FULFILLED,
THOSE WHO PAY NO ATTENTION THINKS ITS NO BIG DEAL.

SOME THINK THEY HAVE PLENTY OF TIME,
I THINK THEY ARE TOTALLY OUT OF THEIR MIND.

EARTHQUAKES, FLOODS, WARS, KILLINGS, NO LOVE,
JUST TO NAME A FEW.
GOD'S WORD SPEAKS THE TRUTH, AND THIS IS NOTHING NEW.

IN THE BEGINNING THE WORLD WAS DESTROYED BY WATER,
THIS TIME THE WORSE WILL GO FARTHER.
FIRE IS THE MOST TO ENDURE,
TO BE SAVED BY HIS GRACE YOU'LL WANT THIS FOR SURE.

GOD'S FORGIVENESS IS TRULY AT HAND,
BUT DON'T WAIT TO LATE AND BE DESTROYED IN THIS LAND.

ON THIS DAY WHEN THE LORD WILL RAISE THE DEAD,
I KNOW OUR SOULS WILL BE SPIRITUALLY LED.

WITH THE ALIVE WITH CHRIST IN THE CLOUDS,
HE WILL SHOUT COME MY CHILDREN, AND IT WILL BE LOUD.

ALL WILL SEE HIM, AND HEAR HIM THAT DAY,
HEAVEN, HEAVEN, FAR, FAR AWAY.

OH! WHAT A BEAUTIFUL DAY THIS WILL BE,
WHEN GOD'S FAITHFULL ONES WILL BE FREE.

Jesus Is Coming Again

I'M SO GLAD JESUS IS COMING BACK AGAIN!
GET READY, WAIT PRAYFULLY, QUICKLY IT WILL ALL END.

TRYING TO STAND THE LAST DAY SAYING,
"LORD PLEASE FORGIVE ME",
NO BREAK, TOO LATE, YOU KNEW WHAT YOUR FAITH WOULD BE.

IF YOU READ YOUR BIBLE, GOD TOLD YOU HOW TO
GET TO THE HOLY LAND.
TOO LATE TO REACH OUT AND ASK FOR GOD'S HAND.

THE SECOND COMING OF CHRIST WAS TOLD WHAT WOULD TAKE
PLACE,
THIS WAS TOLD THE FIRST COMING OF HIS HOLY GRACE.

HE IS COMING IN ALL CLOUDS OF GLORY,
IT WANT BE TIME TO TELL YOU THE OLD, OLD STORY.

THERE WILL BE ONLY TIME FOR THOSE TO GO TO THE
EAST AND SOME TO THE WEST.
THOSE WHO HAVE SERVED HIM WILL TAKE THEIR PEACEFUL REST.

I PRAY THERE WILL BE MANY WHO WILL GO TO THEIR HEAVENLY
HOME,
THERE WILL BE NO MORE STREETS DOWN HERE TO ROME.

He's Coming Soon

I

THE LORD IS SOON TO COME, BUT IT WILL BE A SAD, SAD DAY FOR
SOME.

GOD HAS BEEN PREPARING US FOR A LONG, LONG TIME,
HE KNOWS OUR STRUGGLES, OUR HARDSHIPS,
AND THINGS OF THIS
KIND.

THE BIBLE WHICH HE HAS GIVEN US, THE TOOL
TO MAKE A CHOICE,
IT'S NOT LIKE YOU HAVEN'T BEEN ABLE TO HAVE A VOICE.

YOU SAY YOU WANT TO GO TO HEAVEN TO BE WITH THE LORD,
BUT YOU SEE YOU HAVE TO BE WITH HIM ON ONE ACCORD.

GOD GAVE HIS SON TO SAVE OUR SOULS,
HE'S ALSO GIVEN YOU ANOTHER CHANCE TO GO
DOWN THE RIGHT ROAD.

HE'S EVEN LETTING YOU SEE THE SIGNS ON EARTH
THAT HE'S COMING
SOON.
YOU CAN'T TELL BY LOOKING AT THE STARS, OR THE MOON.

IT'S EVERYTHING IN HIS WORD OF REVELATION ABOUT THE END TIMES,
AND ITS SHOWING DOWN HERE ON EARTH THE SAME SIGNS.

WE AS GOD'S CHILDREN ARE LIVING ON BORROWED TIME,
AND I PRAY THAT WE TAKE OUR SAVIOR'S COMING
SERIOUS IN MIND,

WHO WOULDN'T WANT TO GO TO HEAVEN TO BE
WITH THE LORD?
THE SINS OF THIS WORLD YOU WOULD NEVER HAVE TO AVOID
THERE IS NOTHING BUT PEACE AND JOY FOREVERMORE

YOU WILL NEVER WORRY ABOUT WHAT TO EAT!
FOOD IN ABUNDANCE IT WILL BE A FEAST.

AND WHAT ABOUT SICKNESS, YOU WILL NEVER BE SICK,
YOU WILL NEVER EVEN HAVE TO WORRY ABOUT IT!

AND SOME OF THOSE FAMILY MEMBERS AND FRIENDS THAT YOU
WOULD LOVE TO SEE AGAIN,
THEY WILL RUN AND GREET YOU WITH OUTSTRETCHED HANDS.

ALL THESE WONDERFUL THINGS ARE WAITING FOR YOU,
IF WALKING WITH GOD IS WHO YOU CHOOSE.

This World Is Not My Home

WHEN IT'S ALL SAID AND DONE, AND WHEN THIS LIFE HAVE BEEN RUN,
I WANT TO SEE THE LAST OF THE SETTING SUN, AND SAY TO THIS
WORLD LET THE SAVIOUR COME.

THIS WORLD IS NOT OUR HOME WITH NO LOVE, KILLING AND
DISRESPECTING EACH OTHER,
HOW CAN WE HAVE THE NERVE TO SAY
YOU ARE MY SISTER AND BROTHER.

YOU CAN'T EVEN WALK DOWN THE STREET,
OR GO TO THE GROCERY STORE,
YOU LEAVE THE EXIT, AND GET JUMPED BEFORE YOU GET TO THE DOOR.

WE USE TO BE ABLE TO SIT ON THE PORCH FOR SOME FRESH AIR,
NOW THERE CAN BE A DRIVE BY SHOOTING, AND NO ONE SEEMS TO
CARE.

SATAN IS VERY BUSY IN THIS WORLD TODAY,
OUR ONLY OUT IN THIS SITUATION IS TO CONTINUE TO PRAY.

MORNING, NOON, AND NIGHT, THIS YOU MUST DO,
LET NOTHING SWAY YOU FROM THE LORD, BE FAITHFUL, BE TRUE.

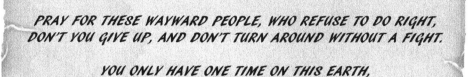

PRAY FOR THESE WAYWARD PEOPLE, WHO REFUSE TO DO RIGHT,
DON'T YOU GIVE UP, AND DON'T TURN AROUND WITHOUT A FIGHT.

YOU ONLY HAVE ONE TIME ON THIS EARTH,
STAY WITH THE LORD, AND GIVE HIM. ALL IT'S WORTH.

In My Darkest Hour

IN MY DARKEST HOUR, I DREAM OF INNER PEACE,
THE PEACE OF BEING FREE.
THE INNER PEACE OF BEING ABLE TO BE ME.

I DREAM OF A PLACE WHERE THERE IS GOD,
THE MAN WHO IS TO SET YOU FREE,
THE MAGNIFICENT MAN WHO DIED FOR YOU AND ME.

IN MY DARKEST HOUR I DREAM OF SO MUCH LOVE,
THE LOVE BETWEEN A MAN AND A WOMAN WHOM GOD PUT TOGETHER,
THE KIND OF LOVE THAT WILL LAST FOREVER AND EVER.

I PRAY IN MY HOURS FOR BEAUTIFUL DAYS AHEAD,
AS I KNEEL ON MY KNEES, AND BOW MY HEAD.

WHAT A WONDERFUL EXPERIENCE TO HAVE LOVE, PEACE,
AND A BETTER LIFE, THAN IN MY DARKEST HOUR,
"GOD SAID", IT CAN ONLY BE OBTAINED THROUGH HIS ALMIGHTY
POWER.

I'M GOING TO KEEP ON PRAYING AND LIFTING MY HEAD TO THEE.
LORD YOU ARE NEAR ME AT MY TIME OF NEED.

LORD IN MY DARKEST HOUR AS I LAY MY HEAD
DOWN TO REST WITH YOU ON MY MIND,
I KNOW I CAN DREAM AND SLEEP AND MY BODY WILL BE FINE.

Going Home

DO NOT CRY FOR ME NOW,
BE HAPPY FOR I AM HEAVEN BOUND.

WHEN I WAS DOWN HERE ON EARTH'
I HAD TO TAKE LIFE FOR WHAT IT WAS WORTH.

WITH ALL THE ACHES, AND ALL THE PAINS,
GOD HELPED ME TO WITHSTAND IT ALL THE SAME.

LIFE DIDN'T DEAL ME THE HIGHEST OF CARDS,
BUT I FEEL GOD IS GOING TO GIVE ME MY REWARDS.

I TRIED TO DO WHAT WAS RIGHT,
IT WAS ALWAYS A STRUGGLE, AND I HAD TO FIGHT.

THE ONLY THING THAT I REGRET,
I WISH MY MOM LOVED ME AS HER CHILD,
LIKE THE REST.

I ALSO HOPE MY GRANDCHILDREN WILL BE REMINDED OF ME,
I WAS A PROUD GRANDMOTHER INDEED.

BE HAPPY I'M GOING TO A BETTER PLACE,
NOTHING WILL MAKE ME HAPPY 'TIL I SEE MY SAVIOUR
FACE TO FACE.

Fighting The Devil

THE PROBLEM IS, WHEN I'M TRYING TO DO WHAT IS RIGHT,
THE DEVIL IS ON MY BACK, MAKING ME PUT UP A FIGHT.

I'M FIGHTING THE INNER PEACE THAT GOD WANTS US TO HAVE,
THE DEVIL IS FIGHTING TO DESTROY WHAT'S UP
FOR HIM TO GRAB.

I LOVE TO GO TO CHURCH, AND PRAISE GOD'S HOLY NAME,
WHEN I STEP OUT SIDE HIS HOUSE, EVERYTHING CHANGE.

I HAVE TO KEEP ON PRAYING, LORD KEEP SATAN AWAY FROM ME,
I'LL KEEP CONFESSING AND PRAYING, LORD!
YOU ARE MY EVERY NEED

LORD, YOU ARE WHAT KEEPS ME SANE EVERYDAY.
IF YOU TAKE YOUR LOVE AWAY FROM ME, I COULD NOT SURVIVE.
NO SHAPE, NO FORM, NO WAY.

TO LIVE WITHOUT YOU EVERY DAY OF MY LIFE,
WOULD BE NOTHING BUT HARDSHIP, PAIN AND STRIFE.

I CAN'T UNDERSTAND WHY PEOPLE DON'T WORSHIP YOU MORE.
LORD YOU ARE THE ONLY KEEPER THAT CAN UNLOCK ANY DOOR.

"Get Behind Me Satan"

SATAN GET BEHIND ME, I WANT TO SERVE THE LORD
YOU HAVE NOTHING TO OFFER ME, YOU ONLY SEEK AND DESTROY.

I WANT A LIFE OF PEACE AND HARMONY, I WANT A LIFE OF HAPPINESS,
AND TO BE FREE,
I WANT TO PRAISE THE LORD, AND ABLE TO BE ME.

GOD OFFERS ALL THESE THINGS IF YOU TRUST AND OBEY HIM,
BUT DEALING WITH SATAN, YOUR LIFE WILL BE VERY DIM.

SATAN LIES, HE STEALS, AND HE TAKES OUR CHILDREN'S LIFE,
BUT IF WE STICK AND TRUST IN GOD, WE WANT GIVE UP WITHOUT A
FIGHT.

ONE DAY I WAS A SINNER, AND DIDN'T KNOW WHICH WAY TO TURN,
I THOUGHT MY LIFE WAS OVER, AND IN HELL I WOULD BURN.

MOM SAID, "TRY JESUS" HE'LL MAKE EVERY THING ALRIGHT,
I TRIED HIM, I PRAYED TO HIM, AND HE BROUGHT ME TO THE LIGHT.

DON'T EVER DEAL WITH ANYTHING DEALING WITH SATAN'S LIFE,
YOU'RE FALL IN THE PITS OF HELL, AND YOU'RE
SOON OR LATER FIND
OUT IT'S NOT RIGHT.

Mom's Death

IT'S HARD TO ACCEPT THAT MOM IS DEAD,
I KNOW IT'S A REALITY BUT I CAN'T GET IT THROUGH MY HEAD.

I'VE BEEN AROUND HER MOST OF THE TIME,
WHEN I WAKE UP IN THE MORNING, SOMETIME THE THOUGHTS ARE IN
MY MIND.

I'M USE TO HER ALWAYS CALLING MY NAME,
LIVING WITHOUT HER IS NOT THE SAME.

ALL THROUGH HER LIFE WE'VE HAD OUR UPS AND DOWN,
SOMETIMES WE WOULDN'T SPEAK, BUT WE ALWAYS CAME AROUND.

SHE KNEW I LOVED HER, AND SHE LOVED ME TOO.
WE WHERE ALWAYS TOLD WE WHERE TWO OF A KIND, SO WHAT
COULD WE DO.

MOM WOULD SAY LORD I'M READY TO COME HOME,
THIS WAS BECAUSE OF HER ACHES AND PAIN OF CANCER,
SHE DID NOT WANT TO GO ON.

I WOULD TELL HER THE LORD WASN'T READY FOR HER YET!
WHEN HE'S READY FOR HER, SHE WOULD TAKE HER REST.

I KNEW THE LORD WOULD COME AND TAKE MOM SOON,
HE CAME AND TOOK MOM AT NOON.

I CAN THINK OF THE THINGS THAT MOM AND I DID TOGETHER,
BUT MOM WILL LIVE IN MY HEART FOREVER AND EVER.

The Millennium 2000

THE MILLENNIUM 2000 IS ALMOST HERE,
SHOULD WE BE RELUCTANT OF WHAT IS NEAR.
SOME SAY WE HAVE NOTHING TO FEAR!

SHOULD WE BE HAPPY OR LISTEN TO WHAT'S BEING SAID.
I KNOW THE LORD, SO I'M NOT THE LEAST AFRAID.

I DO FEEL IT'S A TIME TO REPENT,
FOR ALL THE WRONG DOINGS OF THE LIFE THAT WAS SPENT.

TO DO GOOD, TO PRAY AND BE FAITHFUL FOR YOUR SAKE,
THAT'S THE ONLY WAY YOU CAN ENTER THE PEARLY GATES.

HEAVEN IS THE PLACE I WANT TO BE,
SO COME MILLENNIUM 2000 CENTURY.

Made in the USA
Middletown, DE
30 June 2021